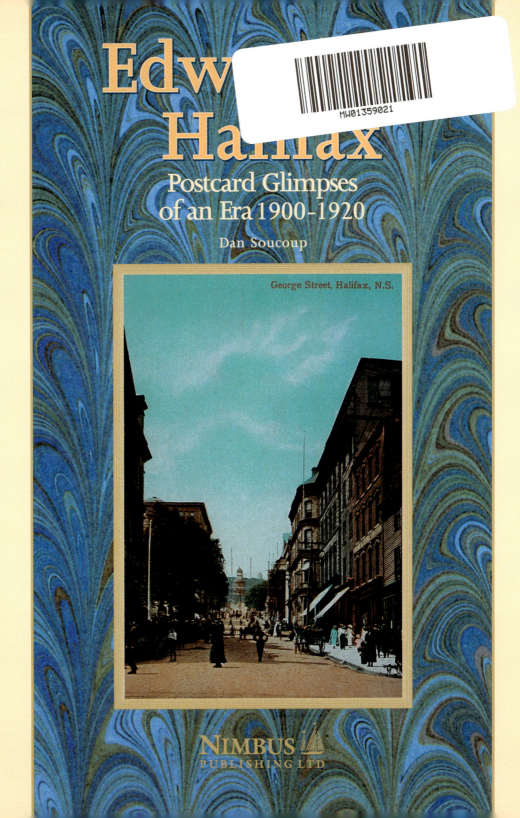

Edw... Halifax

Postcard Glimpses of an Era 1900-1920

Dan Soucoup

George Street, Halifax, N.S.

NIMBUS
PUBLISHING LTD

Copyright © Dan Soucoup, 1998

All rights reserved. No part of this book may be reproduced, stored in a retrieval system or transmitted in any form or by any means without the prior written permission from the publisher, or, in the case of photocopying or other reprographic copying, permission from CANCOPY (Canadian Copyright Licensing Agency), 6 Adelaide Street East, Suite 900, Toronto, Ontario M5C 1H6.

Nimbus Publishing Limited
PO Box 9301, Station A
Halifax, NS B3K 5N5
(902)455-4286

Design: Arthur Carter
Printed and bound by Printcrafters, Inc.

Canadian Cataloguing in Publication Data
Soucoup, Dan, 1949-
Edwardian Halifax
Includes bibliographical references.
ISBN 1-55109-261-1
1. Halifax (N.S.) - History - Pictorial works.
2. Postcards - Nova Scotia - Halifax.   I. Title.

FC2346.37.S6 1998   9716'22503   C98-950192-2
F1039.5.H17S6 1998

Title page: *George St. looking west to the Citadel, c1910*

Nimbus Publishing acknowledges the financial support
of the Canada Council and the Department of Canadian Heritage.

• CONTENTS •

INTRODUCTION
Halifax 1900... iii

CHAPTER ONE
The Harbour and Approaches... 1

CHAPTER TWO
View from the Citadel... 7

CHAPTER THREE
Streetscapes and Civic Life... 13

CHAPTER FOUR
Public Buildings
and Public Life... 25

CHAPTER FIVE
Churches and
Educational Institutions... 33

CHAPTER SIX
Military Scenes... 41

CHAPTER SEVEN
Public Gardens
and other Parks... 49

CHAPTER EIGHT
Point Pleasant Park... 55

CHAPTER NINE
Recreation and the
Northwest Arm... 61

CHAPTER TEN
Neighbourhoods Nearby... 69

CHAPTER ELEVEN
AND CONCLUSION:
Halifax 1920... 77

CHAPTER TWELVE
Edwardian Greeting Cards... 83

Halifax floral card c1908

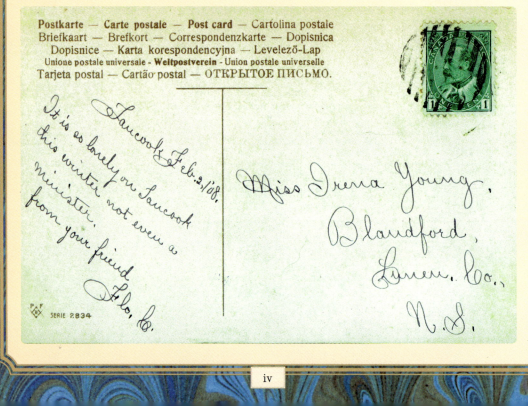

Introduction: Halifax 1900

When a new century dawned almost one hundred years ago, Haligonians felt they had little to celebrate; the British Empire was at war. Although not a world war such as the two to come in the new century, the Boer War of 1899-1902 looked ominous. The Boers promised to bloody Britain's nose.

In January 1900 twenty-five thousand people witnessed the embarkation of the D & E Battalions of the Second Canadian Contingent at the Deep Water Terminal in North End Halifax. With the appalling British losses at Ladysmith, Haligonians were absorbed the entire winter of 1900 with the Boer War and its implications for Britain's far-flung empire. Local newspaper headlines kept them abreast of developments in the far-off war.

Closer to home the Pickford & Black Company offered winter excursions from Halifax to Jamaica for seventy-five dollars return. The Starr Manufacturing Co. Ltd. advertised its Micmac hockey sticks as the highest quality anywhere. Haligonians feeling the winter blues could buy a spring tonic: Dr. Williams' Pink Pills for Pale People.

In 1900 the population of Halifax had reached forty thousand. Since Confederation, however, growth had not kept pace with the rest of Canada, and Halifax dropped from the fourth largest Canadian city to the seventh. Despite a large dockyard at Richmond and its deep water terminal on Upper Water Street, Halifax's port facilities were far from world-class. For more than a century Halifax had thrived on the business of supplying the Imperial Garrison, but this was about to end.

Halifax was in danger of losing its premier port status to other east coast centres when the Royal Dockyard was threatened with closure in 1904. Demands for extensive improvements to the decrepit wharves and sheds along Water Street began immediately. The large steam liners of the North Atlantic run needed concrete berthing structures to adequately off-load their cargo. A plan to upgrade Canada's most eastern terminus was urgently needed.

Nonetheless, Halifax had grown and prospered during the latter part of the nineteenth century. Before Confederation the city had been confined to the area between Citadel Hill and the harbour. By the turn of the century, the waterfront had been extended almost unbroken from Water Street to Richmond. The city had developed south to Inglis Street, along Tower Road to South Street, and as far west as Robie Street. Northwest Halifax had grown along Robie and Windsor Streets as far as Young and Duffus Streets in Richmond.

The most spectacular growth had occurred in the industrial North End, where the suburb of Richmond had developed around the little railway station built in the late 1850s. By 1900 a graving dock, sugar refinery, cotton mill, paint factory, foundry, among other industries dotted the hillside at Richmond and areas farther west to Robie Street and Kempt Road. Four churches served Richmond which was named after the city that supplied the community with flour—Richmond, Virginia.

As the city's North End began to develop with factories and working-class homes, the prominent families along Brunswick and Gottingen Streets began to move to the city's more exclusive residential areas in the South End along Pleasant Street, Inglis Street, and Young Avenue. The South Common fields that had been virtually empty in 1850 were now laced with institutions, including Victoria General Hospital, a Poor House, a School for the Blind, Sacred Heart Convent, an Exhibition Building, and the new Dalhousie College.

At the turn of the century, the North Commons appeared similar to today's Commons with open fields available for recreation, but across from the Armouries on North Park Street, some military sheds still existed. Camp Hill west of Summer Street lay empty, but its role as the city's dump had been discontinued due to the unpleasant odours that infiltrated the Public Gardens nearby.

West of Robie Street, some residential development had occurred between Jubilee and Quinpool Roads and further north along Windsor, Duncan, Lawrence, and Allan Streets. The major movement of the city's population west of the Commons would not take place until the decades between the two world wars.

The modern age of rapid transportation and communication began to appear in Halifax by 1900, signalling the commencement of swift and continual change that would characterize life in the twentieth century. In 1896 Halifax's first electric streetcar service began its route from Mulgrave Park along Upper Water Street to Barrington Street and the city's South End where a terminal was eventually built next to the Nova Scotia Hotel (now the Westin Nova Scotian Hotel). A Coburg Road branch also ran up Spring Garden Road to a terminus near Studley Gate. Early streetcars, built by the Rhodes, Curry & Company of Amherst, were lighted, heated, and propelled by electricity with a seating capacity of twenty-six passengers. It was many years before the familiar electric trolleys gave way to diesel buses.

Although some modes of transportation improved, the conditions of city streets and sidewalks were not satisfactory to the average citizen in Edwardian Halifax. Even more prominent streets like Pleasant Street were covered in mud or dust. With earth sidewalks and no gutters or curbstones, they seemed more

like country lanes than city boulevards. Broken stones had provided the base for most city streets, but the binding material of sand and gravel was often tossed randomly onto the street and would either become mud within hours of heavy rain or dust in intense sunlight.

Rubbish from shopkeepers often littered the streets and women's long skirts easily became soiled during a downtown outing. By 1900 paving stones had been laid across the busy intersections for pedestrians, however, since sidewalk construction and upkeep remained the responsibility of the property owners, concrete, brick, wood, and earth often comprised various sections of the same sidewalk.

Crooked streets became a concern as the city grew dependent upon the streetcar for efficient transportation. Considerable funds were spent to allow straight passage along Lockman Street from Campbell Road to Barrington Street. (Street paving was still decades away. In 1918 a strip of the Bedford Highway outside Halifax became the first paved road in Nova Scotia.)

Electric street lighting had replaced gas and oil lamps in 1886, but private utility companies, such as the Halifax Illuminating and Motor Company, operated for almost a decade before blackouts and electric failures became uncommon occurrences.

The first telephone was installed in Halifax on Dutch Village Road in 1877 at the home of publisher Andrew Mackinlay. Within twenty-five years there were about fifteen hundred phone subscribers in Halifax and Dartmouth. However, during the Edwardian era, the telephone was still regarded as a tool for merchants and professional men, not as a necessity for every home.

Shortly after the turn of the century, the most British of Canadian cities lost its beloved Imperial Garrison and Royal Navy. Halifax had lived in one way or another off the British military for 150 years, when finally the aftermath of Confederation hit home. After 1905, the city would have to find its own way within a new North America, a continent obsessed with inland growth and prosperity. The east coast port with the "finest harbour ever seen" would struggle in the ensuing decades, especially after receiving one of the worst blasts in human history in 1917. Halifax's destiny, like its enduring past, would be linked to the sea.

The New Edwardian Media: Postcards

Early postcards were a fitting medium for the era. The Edwardian fondness for small personal gifts of affection caused the high-calibre and colourful, cards that arrived by post to become the rage. Costing a penny or two and another cent for mailing, postcards were cheap to send and affordable items to collect in postcard albums.

Although often called "the Edwardian craze" because the popularity of postcards peaked during the reign of King Edward VII (1901-1910), these small pictures have their roots in the Victorian age. The world's first picture postcards appeared in Germany in 1869 and were derived from the popular pictorial stationery in use throughout Europe during the nineteenth century. New German printing technology, together with the efforts of the German Post Office, successfully introduced these new pictorial mailing cards to an eager European public.

The development of the postcard in Canada dates back to about 1870, when mail delivery of cards with short business correspondence began. Until 1895 laws prevented advertising slogans or marketing pictures to accompany these business cards, but after high-quality cards printed in Germany began to appear in Canada, changes in postal legislation allowed for postcard advertising. A rush of colourful and clever business cards appeared immediately in Canada and the postcard's popularity remained in vogue throughout Europe and the United States well into the twentieth century. Postcards became so popular by 1909 that the German Post Office had roving Postmen selling them in restaurants and open-air marketplaces. Senders of greetings could complete the transaction by dropping their messages into a portable letter-box strapped to each Postman's back.

By 1900, general interest postcards with lovely Canadian scenes and beautiful decorations bearing Christmas and birthday greetings appeared in shops and stores. A Scottish company, J. V. Valentine and Sons, produced the finest quality postcards in Canada and by 1912 had produced around twenty thousand Canadian views. The photographs were shot in black and white, then exquisitely hand-coloured and lithographed, initially in Germany, and later in Britain and North America.

Like television today, picture postcards were a popular and direct media that recorded the new century, its people, as well as its exciting events. Newspapers still relied heavily on drawings and the printed word; postcards often delivered a stark and pointed picture that captured a moment in a way that words could not. Postcards also focused on beautiful and serene scenes, creating demand for such colourful images to be sent to others as small gifts of affection.

In the Maritimes, where tourism was in its infancy, postcards served as its first tools. Familiar scenes of the most famous sites and landscapes were quickly produced to capture the traveller's eye. Halifax was one of the most popular destinations on the east coast and within the first decade of the twentieth century, more than one thousand images were mass-produced.

We are indeed fortunate for this wealth of photographic cards that reveals wonderful details of Edwardian Halifax. The enticing collection presented here is only a small representation of the many nostalgic images still kept by keen or unknown collectors in dusty photo albums and old chests.

While the odd picture from the post-1920 era has been included here to demonstrate changes or highlight the evolution of Halifax's landscape, the majority of the images are pre-World War I except for the tragic and bleak pictures of the Halifax Explosion, which capture an important event in Halifax history.

With a new century approaching and the impending 250th anniversary of the settlement of Halifax, it is fascinating to look back to a period that seems so far removed from our own today. Yet, we see familiar sights to remind us that this century's first decade also shaped the modern era.

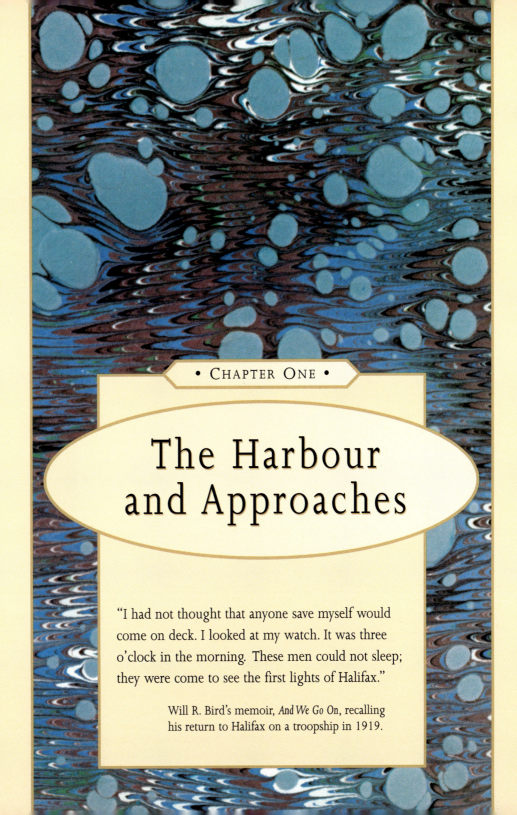

• CHAPTER ONE •

The Harbour and Approaches

"I had not thought that anyone save myself would come on deck. I looked at my watch. It was three o'clock in the morning. These men could not sleep; they were come to see the first lights of Halifax."

Will R. Bird's memoir, *And We Go On*, recalling his return to Halifax on a troopship in 1919.

• Edwardian Halifax •

Entrance to Halifax Harbour c1912

One of the world's great natural harbours was large enough to hold the entire British navy, and indeed, during the War of 1812 and the two world wars, Halifax Harbour nearly did. More than 8 mi. (13 km) in length, it was often called the long harbour of Halifax. In the early 1700s, a French naval engineer, De Labat, marvelled that the entire harbour and basin could easily hold one thousand vessels and become a military and naval stronghold. The Great Harbour, called "Chebucto" by the Mi'kmaq, boomed with activity in war times but always suffered a reversal of fortune during peacetime.

General View of Halifax c1912

Visible in the background of the seaport's historic waterfront are the twin steeples of St. Matthew's Church and St. Mary's Cathedral. The high point in the background is occupied by the signal mast of the Citadel. The town's first settlements began along this shoreline after Cornwallis discovered his initial choice at Point Pleasant was too exposed to south-east gales. Within a few years of this photograph, Halifax would be awash in World War I, and the first of many naval convoy destined for the European front would exit from this site.

"Reflections," Halifax Harbour c1912

Fishing boats sit off Georges Island. One of the deepest natural harbours found along the east coast, Halifax Harbour was known to the Mi'kmaq as the "biggest harbour" and to Samuel de Champlain as "a good safe bay." Col. Edward Cornwallis, upon arriving in 1749, dashed off a dispatch to the First Lord of the Admiralty, recalling that his officers had called Chebucto harbour "the finest they have ever seen." Military figures would continue to see immense value in the harbour's size and location, as in 1941, when the British rear admiral S. S. Bonham-Carter cited Halifax Harbour as "probably the most important port in the world."

Halifax from Georges Island c1908

Despite its many military installations, Georges Island was a popular picnic spot for Haligonians in the early 1900s. In the mid-1700s the historic island contained the remains of Duc D'Anville whose ill-fated voyage to recapture Louisbourg ended in tragedy and despair in Bedford Basin. The smokestack in the background to the right is the Nova Scotia Sugar Refinery at Richmond. A lone schooner lies at anchor, perhaps waiting to unload West India sugar.

• Edwardian Halifax •

Georges Island from Halifax c1918

This view was taken from Pier 21 looking across to the Dartmouth shore at Woodside. On the left is the smokestack and modern brick structure of the Acadia Sugar Refining Company, which had begun processing sugar at Woodside in 1884. It burned in 1912 and was rebuilt, but rationing forced the company to close during World War II. To the right of Georges Island is the Imperial Oil Refinery. Begun in 1916 near the former Fort Clarence site, the refinery expanded immediately after World War I and soon employed a large work force that created the busy suburb known as Imperoyal.

Yacht Racing, Halifax Harbour c1908

Off shore from the Royal Nova Scotia Yacht Squadron (RNSYS), stretching across the background, is the largest island in the harbour, McNabs Island, immortalized in Thomas Raddall's celebrated novel *Hangman's Beach*. Canada's first sailing regatta took place in the harbour in 1826 as part of a welcoming ceremony for Lord Dalhousie. In addition to sailing competitions among the British naval officers, Mi'kmaq raced their canoes to Georges Island and back.

Children Playing at Greenbank c1910

This wonderful picture of a glorious summer day shows four children and four sails in Halifax Harbour. The vista is from the shore near Black Rock Beach where, today, modern container piers and grain elevators have replaced the serene seaside neighbourhood that had developed between the city's waterfront and Point Pleasant Park.

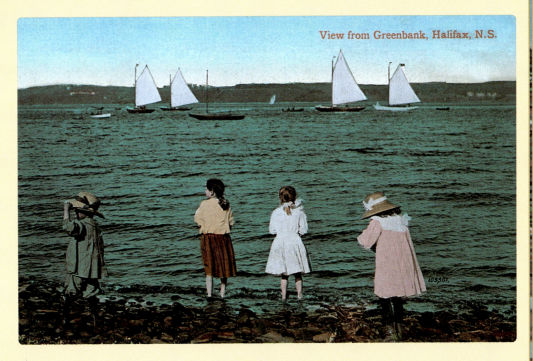

Halifax Ocean Terminals from the Harbour c1920

This scene differs dramatically from the earlier pre-war picture of children playing at pristine Greenbank. This is likely an artist's conception of the projected port terminal that was built around Greenbank in the city's South End after the 1917 Halifax Explosion destroyed much of the North End waterfront. By 1930 this depiction would include the incoming railway tracks from Fairview, the grain elevators, and the Nova Scotian Hotel. Georges Island appears at the bottom of the picture.

• EDWARDIAN HALIFAX •

Yachting in Halifax Harbour, N.S.

Yachting in Halifax Harbour c1907

Small vessels and fishing dories lie idle on the left against the Dartmouth shore while the sloop works its way towards the Halifax waterfront. Until the harbour became crowded with naval vessels and large shipping liners, Halifax Harbour was an ideal venue for yachting and competitive racing. After 1931, the new quay opposite Georges Island allowed the world's largest naval vessels and ocean liners to dock. During the 1940s the largest naval build-up in Canadian history occurred. Eventually, yacht racing and pleasure yachting became more enjoyable pastimes in the protected surroundings of Bedford Basin and the Northwest Arm.

Ocean Liner in Port c1945

This aerial photograph was taken by the Royal Canadian Air Force (RCAF) over Halifax Harbour. By World War II, Halifax's Ocean Terminals were constructed along the harbour between the city and Point Pleasant Park. The Nova Scotian Hotel is on the right. In the background, the substantial residential development between Inglis Street and Point Pleasant Park is visible. The liner is docked along the 2,007-ft (612-m) long Quay Wall that in 1939 berthed three American battleships—*New York*, *Texas*, and *Arkansas*. On the far left is the huge grain elevator that held countless tons of Canadian wheat that were loaded onto cargo ships on their way to overseas markets.

Ocean Liner and The Nova Scotian Hotel, Halifax, N.S.—R.C.A.F. Photo.—10.

• CHAPTER TWO •

View from the Citadel

"There were twelve warships in port and all, hulls, spars and funnels, were picked out with electric lights. The effect against the inky blackness of the harbour was magical."

L. M. Montgomery, Halifax,
November 23, 1901.

Halifax from the Citadel c1909

Looking east, the old Town Clock, George Street, the harbour, and the Dartmouth shore fill this vista. While a few vessels are evident, one hundred years earlier the harbour had been packed with shipping and naval activity that produced, in the words of one visitor, "a forest of spars." By this time Halifax had lost a good deal of its international commerce through the decline of the wooden shipping trade. However, within a few years, the harbour would be alive again with convoys of supply and relief ships that would navigate the North Atlantic during World War I.

The Citadel at Night c1909

The old Town Clock is dark, but light appears in two windows in the clock's basement. Likely the photograph was taken during the day and tinted by an artist to produce the twilight effect, a common practice in the early years of the postcard trade.

Georges Island from the Citadel c1910

From the north-east, looking off to Georges and McNabs islands, the twin steeples of St. Mary's and St. Matthew's Churches are visible in front of McNabs. Tiny Georges Island is only 800 yd. (732 m) out from the shore of downtown Halifax. It was fortified as soon as Halifax was established in 1749. Georges Island became Halifax's first powder storage magazine for the king's ships. After the War of 1812, the twelve hundred barrels of gunpowder were moved to within the stone earthworks of Citadel Hill.

Halifax from Citadel.

From the Citadel c1918

A few years later and almost from the same viewpoint, little has changed, although the old Town Clock has been painted. Cannons point east, and a horse-drawn carriage appears on the hillside road to the right. On the left, at the corner of Brunswick and George Streets, stands the Engine House, which was considered the city's central fire station and "the best public building owned by the city" after its construction in 1871.

HARBOR AND CITY CLOCK, HALIFAX, N. S.

• EDWARDIAN HALIFAX •

Georges Island at Night c1906

This is the classic view of Halifax Harbour looking south-east from the slope of Citadel Hill to Georges and McNabs Islands. Only the top floor of the Halifax County Academy on Brunswick Street is visible. The outline of St. David's Presbyterian Church—built in 1868 as the Grafton Street Methodist Church—as well as the spire of St. Mary's Cathedral, appear silhouetted against the water. Quite possibly this is a tinted photograph to give the appearance of evening, a process which involved creating a moon and colouring windows yellow.

Old Town Clock c1906

This view looks east from the Citadel. During the late 1700s Prince Edward, Duke of Kent, became commander-in-chief of Halifax and ordered a clock placed on Citadel Hill to overlook the town so that the hour could be conveniently seen by the townsfolk. Ordered from London, the Old Town Clock was installed in 1803 after arriving on HMS *Dart*. The Prince left Halifax before witnessing the installation. Today the Old Town Clock is one of the city's most prominent landmarks.

Old Town Clock c1910

In this view from Brunswick Street, on the eastern slope of the Citadel sits one of the most familiar scenes in Canada: the Old Town Clock. Intended as a Garrison Clock, it marked the many military and civilian events in the historic naval station of Halifax, a port immortalized by Rudyard Kipling as "the warden of the Honour of the North."

The Old Town Clock and the Citadel c1914

Halifax's celebrated historic site has remained a fixture of the city's landscape through almost two centuries. It even kept time during the Halifax Explosion of 1917. The familiar clock served as the subject of Joseph Howe's 1836 poetic ode to "Thou grave old Time Piece" that, according to Howe, remained steadfast through life's unpredictable storms and was a great "example to all the idle chaps about the town." Since few people owned watches in the early 1800s, the clock's placement at the top of George Street was seen as an important public duty to ensure an orderly and well-run town.

Aerial View of the Citadel, Halifax, Nova Scotia.—23.

Aerial View of the Citadel c1930

Facing the west end, this view takes in Quinpool Road and the Northwest Arm. The western suburbs had begun to expand toward the Arm by 1930, yet open undeveloped fields are clearly visible beyond the present Connaught Avenue. South of Jubilee Road, much residential development had taken place. In the centre of the photograph, the North Commons were still without many of today's well-known structures, except for the Camp Hill buildings.

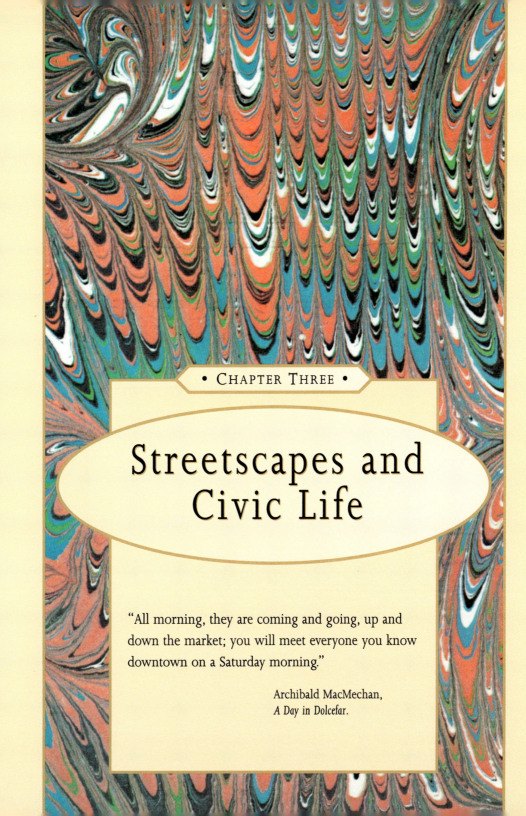

• CHAPTER THREE •

Streetscapes and Civic Life

"All morning, they are coming and going, up and down the market; you will meet everyone you know downtown on a Saturday morning."

Archibald MacMechan,
A Day in Dolcefar.

BIRD'S-EYE VIEW LOOKING NORTH, HALIFAX, N.S.

Bird's-Eye View Looking North c1918

This Halifax scene is from the waterfront. In the early 1900s, the public was fascinated with the concept of flight, and the use of aerial photography by means of cameras mounted on balloons or steeple wires was in vogue. This photo was taken probably in the same manner near the waterfront looking northwest across the city. In the centre of the picture are Government House, the twin steeples of St. Matthew's and St. Mary's cathedral, and Citadel Hill.

Looking North from St. Matthews Steeple, Halifax, N.S.

Barrington Street Looking North from St. Matthew's Steeple c1913

From Salter Street south to Point Pleasant Park, Barrington Street, an important area for commerce, was called Pleasant Street in pre-World War I Halifax. By the early 1900s, Barrington (Pleasant) Street had become home to a number of important Halifax institutions, including the Academy of Music in the foreground on the right. On the opposite side heading north are St. Mary's Glebe House, Farquhar Brothers, Brander Morris Building, St. Mary's Hall (St. Mary's Young Men Total Abstinence and Benevolent Society), City Club, and the Church of England Institute.

Barrington Street North from Sackville Street c1910

A fascinating yet uneasy mix of the nineteenth and twentieth centuries in which three modes of transportation compete for their rightful place on Halifax streets. The electric streetcar had replaced the horse-drawn railway in 1896 and dominated the centre lane of Barrington Street. Banished to the street gutter on the right is the dependable nineteenth-century horse and carriage. The clunker heading north on the left side of Barrington Street is an early automobile whose later versions would dominate twentieth-century transportation.

Barrington Street c1918

This view is north from Sackville Street a few years later, revealing the hustle and bustle of Halifax street life. More revealing is the absence of the horse and buggy; the automobile is prevalent. The second decade of the twentieth century had introduced other changes to Halifax life, including ladies' fashion. Women's hemlines began to rise.

Barrington Street, Halifax, N.S.

Barrington Street Trolley c1908

South from the entrance to St. Paul's Church, the electric streetcar service was visible. It began in 1896, and the early cars that were built in Amherst had patent gates on each side to prevent passengers from falling out. The tall Gothic building on the left was constructed in 1893 for the George M. Smith & Company, a dry goods firm. The contrasting smooth and rough-textured stonework was the creation of well-known local architect, James Charles Dumaresq. Next door, the light brick and granite Kaiser Building was built about the same time for dentist Edmund Ennis.

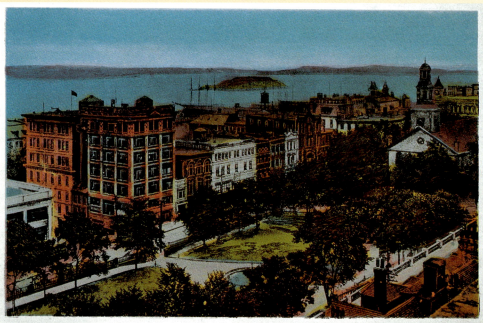

"The Parade", Barrington St., Halifax, Nova Scotia, Canada.

The Grand Parade, Barrington Street c1920

This tinted photograph showing St. Paul's Church and the Grand Parade was probably taken from Moirs Limited, the large confectionery manufacturer that established itself on the Grafton Street site in the 1860s. The Grand Parade was laid out in 1749 and used by the militia as a drill parade. It eventually fell into a dilapidated state until improvements in the late 1800s turned it into the handsome common of Halifax's pre-eminent public square.

Across Barrington Street c1935

From inside the Grande Parade and down George Street, a three-masted schooner is just visible in the harbour. Part way down George Street at Hollis, the cupola of the Post Office is visible. Next door the clock tower of the Custom House reveals that the photograph was taken at 1:45 P.M. The building on the right is the Cragg Building, home to the Cragg Bros.' hardware business. At the turn of the century this seven-storey structure was advertised as the tallest commercial building in the Maritimes; its rooftop offered "the best view of Halifax and vicinity."

George and Barrington Streets from the "Parade," Halifax, Nova Scotia.—35.—A. R. Cogswell and Co., Photo.

Hollis Street Looking North c1908

From Hollis at Prince Street the Post Office is visible on the right. The first structure to the right is the Union Bank building, which opened in 1856 during the shipping prosperity of the Crimean War. The second floor of this building became the first campus of the Victoria School of Art and Design under painter George Harvey who served as principal from 1887 until 1894. Today the site is occupied by the Bank of Nova Scotia.

HOLLIS STREET LOOKING NORTH. HALIFAX, N.S.

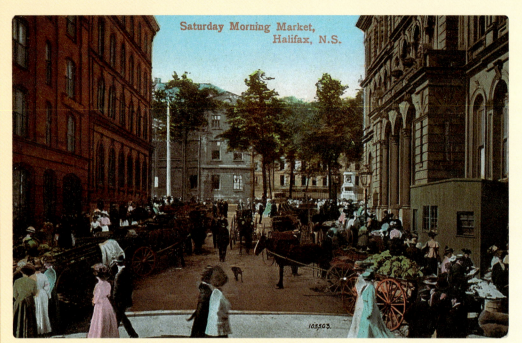

Saturday Morning Market c1905

A "flesh" or "meat" market opened in Halifax as early as 1750, and soon green produce from Acadian farms also appeared. The original site was on George Street. Although a market building had been constructed in 1851 on Bedford Row, the country people refused to use it and sold their produce in this open-air site called Cheapside. This photograph looks west to Hollis Street. Province House is noticeable in the background.

Scene in the Green Market c1906

Every Wednesday and Saturday morning the most colourful place in Halifax was undoubtedly the Green Market strung along Bedford Row to George Street and around the Post Office. Good fresh food at low prices appealed to Halifax citizens, and the picturesque commotion of jostling crowds wandering among the carts, baskets, and stalls invited interesting comments by visitors to the city. Many of the permanent merchants nearby were not amused and often complained to the City Fathers about becoming surrounded by street hawkers from the countryside two times every week.

Green Market c1907

This vibrant scene from the last years of one of Halifax's oldest institutions had become a famous landmark by the turn of the century. In 1907, the *Halifax Herald* reported that the outside Green Market would soon end. Concern had been raised by the Health Department about selling food on the sidewalk. Even when the new market house opened uptown, many country vendors refused to drag their goods up the hill and had to be escorted by police officers away from the historic Cheapside.

Green Market, Halifax, N.S.

City Market c1925

Once loaded carts could be hauled from the ferry up the steep hill by motor car or truck, the location of the city's Green Market could be moved from its controversial site cluttered around the city's permanent merchants on Bedford Row and George Street. In 1913 the new Market Building was begun at a cost of $150,000 on Albemarle Street, which is now known as Market Street. Opened in 1916 on the former site of the police station at Brunswick and Buckingham Streets, the new City Market remained a fixture in the city's commercial life until urban renewal efforts in the late 1960s razed many of the buildings around Market Street.

City Market, Halifax, N. S.

St. Mary's Young Men c1911

Abstinence from alcohol was an important social issue in the first decade of the 1900s and many religious organizations formed anti-alcoholic chapters. Formed in 1891, the St. Mary's Young Men's Total Abstinence and Benevolent Society was a Catholic league that often held marches and parades in favour of a total ban on alcoholic consumption. This photograph shows the society marching south on Pleasant Street with the spire of St. Mary's Cathedral in the background.

Intercolonial Railway (I.C.R.) Station and the King Edward Hotel c1908

Completed in 1877 on Upper Water Street at the foot of North Street, the Station was the ocean terminus for the Intercolonial Railway from Quebec. The King Edward Hotel appears on the left. Outside the station, the cab drivers jockeyed for customers and, according to Hugh MacLennan in *An Orange From Portugal*, these drivers "would mass behind a heavy anchor chain and terrify travellers with bloodcurdling howls as they bid for fares." The station was destroyed by the 1917 Explosion. Instead of rebuilding, a new rail line was blasted out of the rocks from Fairview to the South End, where Union Station was constructed along with new ocean terminals.

Queen Hotel c1930

The best hotels, including the Halifax Hotel and the Albion Hotel, were located on Hollis Street near the business district. The Queen Hotel, originally called the International Hotel, was also situated on the east side of Hollis Street between Salter and Sackville Streets. A fire in 1873 destroyed much of the original wooden structure, but the hotel was rebuilt and renamed in 1886 under the ownership of A. B. Sheraton. Close to Province House, the Queen Hotel was a favourite haunt for politicians and became known as "the after hours Province House."

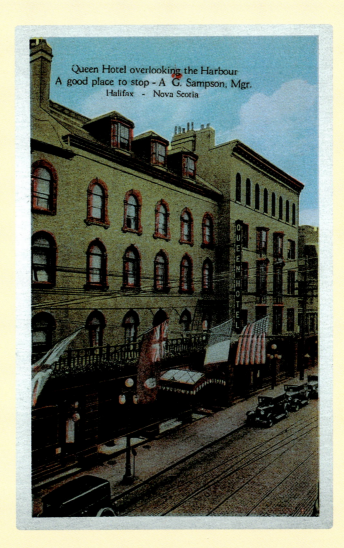

• EDWARDIAN HALIFAX •

Lord Nelson Hotel c1930

This grand hotel at Spring Garden Road and South Park Street was constructed in the late 1920s in uptown Halifax, away from the city centre but close to the Public Gardens, city parks and playgrounds such as the Wanderers' Grounds and the Commons. The hotel's location created a serene, countrylike atmosphere for guests and quickly became a chic address for both visitors and Haligonians. Halifax's first radio station, CHNS, operated from the hotel's top floor before relocating to Tobin Street.

The Waterfront from Upper Water Street c1906

An alluring view south from the grain elevator near the foot of North Street reveals docks and warehouses that remained unchanged for almost a century. The last Imperial troops left Halifax in 1906 leaving a distressing lull in harbour activity. At mid-century the narrow winding Water Street with its cluster of small wharves, warehouses, dingy sheds, and taverns would eventually be swept away by urban renewal efforts to modernize the city.

From the Grain Elevator c1907

This view is north toward the sugar refinery at Richmond. Halifax's first grain elevator, built in 1882, was destroyed by fire. Rebuilt in 1899 on a site near the I.C.R. Station, this view reveals the mixture of industrial and residential development that had sprung up along Halifax's north waterfront since Confederation. With its smokestack, the Nova Scotia Sugar Refinery was Halifax's tallest building in 1907 and Richmond's major industry. Completed in 1881 at the foot of Young Street, the refinery stood nine stories tall and produced tons of refined sugar for Canadian markets. It was destroyed in the Halifax Explosion and was never rebuilt.

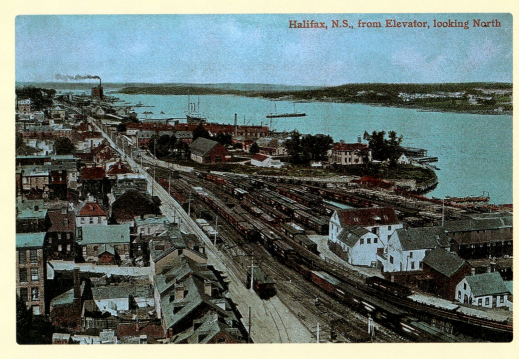

Halifax, N.S., from Elevator, looking North

View West from Grain Elevator c1912

From the same elevator, a view inland to the north-west shows a trolley on Lockman Street at the bottom of the picture. Directly above on Brunswick Street, St. John's Presbyterian Church is visible. Next door, heading north, is St. Patrick's Girls New High School. This large brick structure, erected during the first decade of the 1900s, was the second Catholic school on Brunswick Street. Far in the distance to the right, is the Deaf and Dumb Institution, which had been constructed in 1895 on the east side of Gottingen Street near North Street.

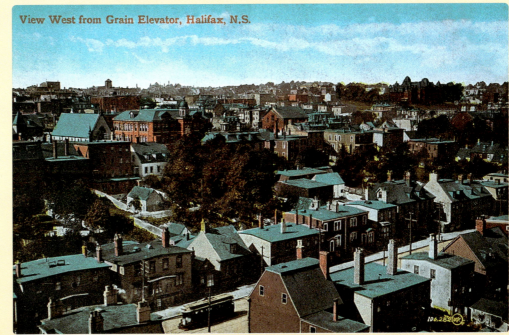

View West from Grain Elevator, Halifax, N.S.

• Edwardian Halifax •

George Street, looking East, Halifax, N.S.

George Street, Halifax, N.S.

George Street looking east c1911

A streetscape in the opposite direction from the view on the right reveals a quiet afternoon in downtown Halifax. George Street appears less than bustling although two sets of horse and carriage are visible above the Grand Parade. City Hall is on the far left.

George Street c1908

Looking west from the harbour afforded this view of the Town Clock and Citadel Hill. On the north-east corner of George and Granville Streets, one column of the newly constructed Bank of Commerce (1906) building is visible. The Dennis Building appears above the treetops on the right. George Street was cluttered with carts since the city's Green Market was located nearby.

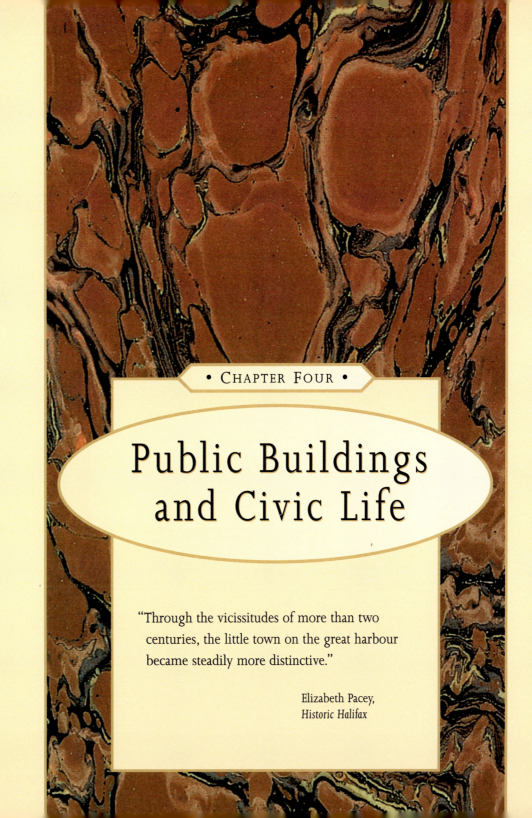

• CHAPTER FOUR •

Public Buildings and Civic Life

"Through the vicissitudes of more than two centuries, the little town on the great harbour became steadily more distinctive."

Elizabeth Pacey,
Historic Halifax

Government House c1912

This structure was the third Government House. The construction took more than five years before Governor Sir John Wentworth was able to move into the fine Georgian structure in 1805. Final costs were three times the projected budget of ten thousand pounds, a staggering sum for the early 1800s. Government House has provided lodging and hosted splendid celebrations for numerous lieutenant-governors throughout the last two centuries. The original entrance was on the east side facing Hollis Street. Today, the main entrance faces Barrington Street as it does in this picture.

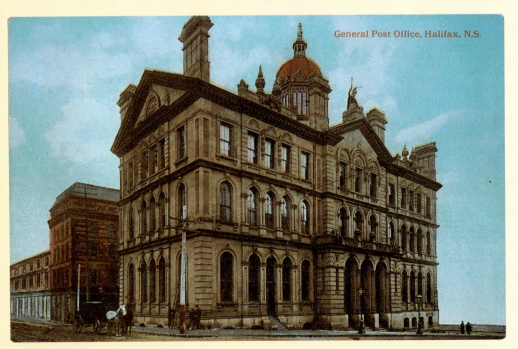

Post Office c1905

Construction on the Post Office began prior to Confederation by the Nova Scotia government. The intention was that a new Provincial Building (Province House was then known as the Provincial Building) would house the Post Office, Custom House, and Railway Department. Following Confederation the building was acquired by the federal government, but only after protracted negotiations due to anti-Confederation feelings led to an eighty thousand dollar payment to the province.

Province House c1910

As seen from Prince Street, this National Historic Site is the oldest Canadian legislative building in use today. On the left is the statue of Joseph Howe with the Granville streetscape in the background. Since its construction in 1819, Province House is perhaps the most important political institute in Canada, playing host to numerous political events such as Joseph Howe's famous freedom of the press speech in 1835, the fight for Responsible Government in the 1840s, and the Confederation debates of the 1960s. Refurbished many times, this photograph shows the handsome Georgian structure covered with the grime and soot from the coal dust of Victorian Halifax.

Joseph Howe's Monument c1911

Located in the south yard of Province House, the statue faces the harbour with Prince Street in the background. The legendary Joseph Howe was Nova Scotia's most influential political figure. He began his career in Halifax in the 1820s as a newspaper editor. Controversy and political turmoil follow his turbulent career in public office, but his courage and spirited defence of the oppressed made him a Canadian folk hero and Nova Scotia's best known statesman.

Post Office c1918

This magnificent edifice is one of Nova Scotia's finest public buildings and a triumph of the classical Italianate style. Situated at Cheapside on the corner of Hollis and George Streets, the Post Office has served many functions since it opened in 1871, including Post Office, Custom House, Provincial Museum, Bank of Canada, and RCMP Headquarters. Today it is home to the Art Gallery of Nova Scotia.

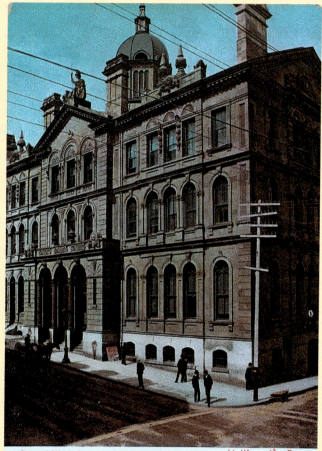

Post Office, Corner of Hollis and George Sts.   Halifax. N. S.

• EDWARDIAN HALIFAX •

City Hall c1910

Declared a National Historic Site in 1984, City Hall has witnessed more than a century of democracy since it was erected out of granite and Nova Scotia freestone in 1890. This picture shows the famous building from across the Grand Parade at the south end near St. Paul's Church. Only after Dalhousie College left the site for a new location in the city's west end did the City Fathers arrange to quit their cramped quarters on George Street for this celebrated locale on the north end of the Grand Parade.

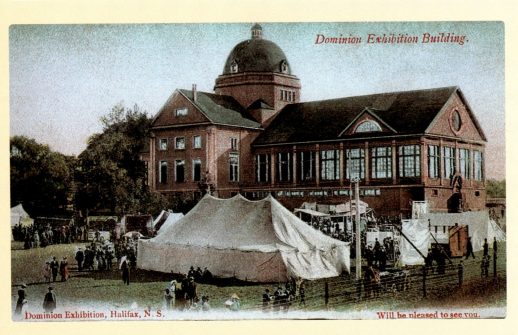

Dominion Exhibition Building c1906

This building was erected in 1897 by the joint efforts of the City of Halifax and the Nova Scotia government at Willow Park on Windsor Street. An Implements Building, Agricultural and Dairy Building, Horse and Cattle Building, and a number of other structures were built as well to comprise a major Provincial Exhibition Centre. Behind the Dominion Building was a grandstand with a four thousand spectator capacity and a half-mile racing track. Thousands attended the annual exhibitions and sporting events until the Halifax Explosion destroyed much of the complex.

The Infirmary Hospital c1933

Begun in 1886 as a small private hospital on Barrington and Blowers Streets, mostly through the efforts of the distinguished Dartmouth surgeon Edward Farrell, the Infirmary remained a small institution throughout the early decades of the twentieth century. Only thirty beds in total could be used during the Halifax Explosion. This photograph shows the new facility after it was opened on Queen Street in 1933 administered by the Sisters of Charity. A private facility until 1948, the Infirmary remained a critical part of Halifax's medical establishment until it closed in the late 1990s.

The Infirmary, Queen St., Halifax, Nova Scotia.   12

Academy of Music c1920

Built of brick faced with stucco, the Academy of Music opened in 1877 on Pleasant (Barrington) Street with a concert by the Halifax Philharmonic Union and the Boston Philharmonic Club of Instrumentalists. One of the first public buildings in Halifax to be lighted by electricity, the Academy of Music served Halifax for more than fifty years as the major entertainment centre, hosting events as diverse as grand opera and ballet, to local repertory performances and vaudeville. In 1900 the first picture show, titled "The Biography," was screened here. "The Biography" was a series of still photographs from the Boer War in South Africa.

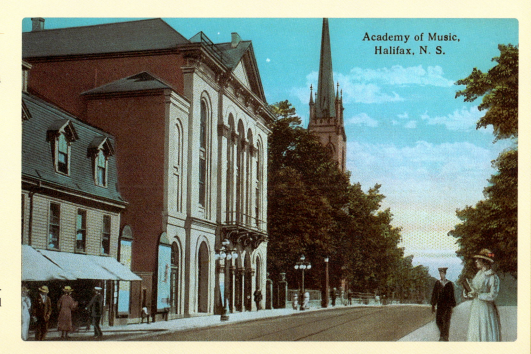

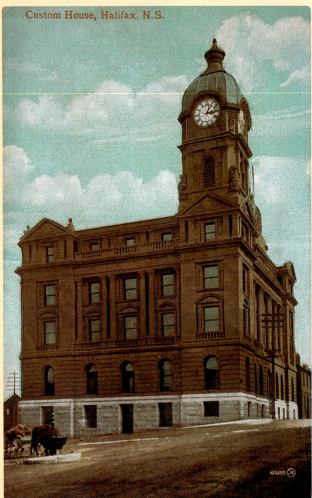

Custom House c1908

Called the new Custom House, this structure was built in the early 1900s behind the Post Office on the former market site at Bedford Row. Constructed entirely of granite and freestone, the clock tower became a welcome sight for Haligonians around the waterfront who were unable to see the Old Town Clock on the Citadel. The Custom House had been located within the Post Office, but by the 1890s demand for a separate building led federal authorities to finance and construct this edifice that remained an important element of the city's architecture until its demise in the 1970s when it was demolished to make way for an expansion of the nearby Bedford Row Post Office.

Victoria General Hospital c1906

This red brick structure first appeared on the South Commons at Tower Road in 1859 as a charity hospital for the ill and the poor. Named in honour of Queen Victoria in 1887, the Victoria General was reorganized under provincial government jurisdiction to serve the entire province. By the early 1900s, the Victoria General had begun to make the transition from a nineteenth-century charity institution that dealt inefficiently with disease to a twentieth-century medical hospital committed to the treatment of illness based on scientific knowledge.

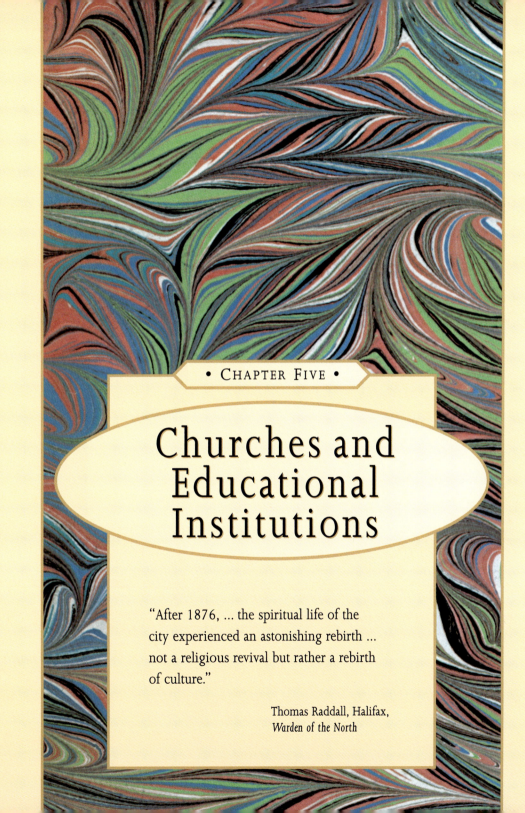

• CHAPTER FIVE •

Churches and Educational Institutions

"After 1876, ... the spiritual life of the city experienced an astonishing rebirth ... not a religious revival but rather a rebirth of culture."

Thomas Raddall, Halifax,
Warden of the North

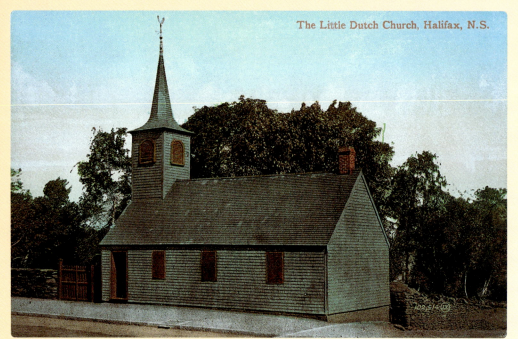

The Little Dutch Church c1912

Canada's first Lutheran church was erected on Brunswick Street in the North End in 1756. European Protestants—mostly German, and some French, Dutch, and Swiss—immigrated to Halifax when it was first settled and established a tiny log house for community gatherings. The small 20 x 20 ft. (6x6 m) meeting house with a capacity for seventy-five people served as the area's school, church, and social centre. Still standing today, the Little Dutch Church was also affectionately known in the North End as "the Chicken-Cock Church" due to its rooster weather vane. A small historic cemetery lies directly behind the church.

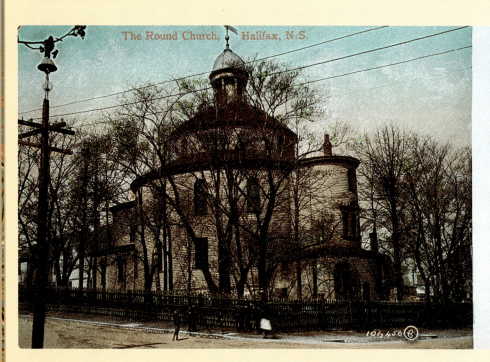

St. George's Round Church c1910

This view from Brunswick Street shows one of the most unique and historic structures in Canada. A National Historic Site, St. George's Anglican Church in the Round was begun in 1800 with assistance from Prince Edward, Duke of Kent, after many of the North End residents became members of the Church of England. St. Paul's was unable to handle the growing northern suburbs and St. George's was established as a separate parish in 1827, and consecrated the same year by Bishop John Inglis.

St. Paul's Church c1910

Halifax's oldest standing building and Canada's earliest Protestant church, as it appeared in the early 1900s. Facing the Grand Parade from its south end, the pine timbers and oak frames of this historic landmark were shipped from Boston at a cost of one thousand pounds. Services were first held in 1750. Modelled after Marybone Chapel in London, services were held for Dissenters and Mi'kmaq in the early pioneer settlement since other religious institutions were not readily available.

Interior of St. Mary's Cathedral c1907

Although established as an "official" Protestant settlement in 1749, a significant number of Catholics arrived in pioneer Halifax and a Catholic Church (St. Peter's) first appeared in 1784, after penal laws against Catholics were repealed. The foundation stone for St. Mary's Cathedral was first laid by Bishop Edmund Burke in 1820 with improvements made throughout the nineteenth century. By 1900, Catholics comprised about 42 per cent of the entire population of Halifax, and they exerted considerable influence on the city's cultural and political life.

St. Mary's Cathedral from St. Matthews c1908

View from St. Matthew's Church on Pleasant (Barrington) Street shows the dressed granite spire of St. Mary's, one of the tallest in the region. Along with Citadel Hill, the twin spires of St. Mary's and St. Matthew's dominated Halifax's skyline until the high-rise construction boom of the late 1900s. The startling Gothic facade pictured here was completed in 1874 under Archbishop Thomas Connolly's episcopate and dramatically changed the cathedral's more reserved Georgian roots. Next door is the St. Mary's Glebe House. Just visible in the lower right corner of the picture is the Academy of Music.

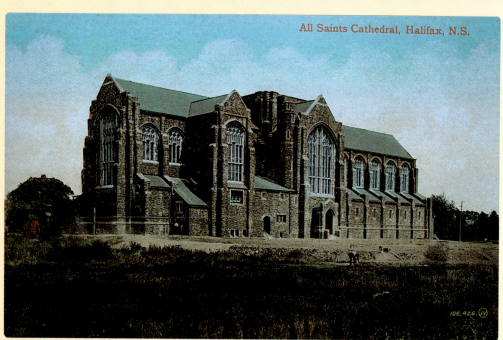

All Saints Cathedral c1911

Built in 1910 on the city's Exhibition Grounds on Tower Road, All Saints Cathedral became the ecclesiastical centre for Nova Scotia. The striking feature is the absence of a spire, yet the Gothic revival style is considered an architectural triumph. All Saints was the last large public building in Halifax to be constructed out of a heavy dark and grey ironstone that was taken from the Queen's Quarries across the Northwest Arm near Purcells Cove. Despite its stone exterior, All Saints Cathedral sustained massive structural damages during the Halifax Explosion.

Deaf and Dumb Institution c1908

This fifty thousand dollar brick structure was erected in 1895 at a site on Gottingen Street known as Cunard's Fields, between North and Uniacke Streets. Education for the deaf had begun in Halifax in 1855 when Scottish immigrant William Grey instructed two pupils in a small room on Argyle Street. In 1857, with assistance from the Nova Scotia Legislature, a boarding school for the deaf was established in an old wooden building on Gottingen Street. Unique to the Maritimes, the school was gradually enlarged to accommodate an increasing number of pupils until it was demolished in 1895 to make way for the new institution pictured here.

School for the Blind c1909

First erected in 1869 on Morris Street, between South Park Street and Tower Road, the School for the Blind became one of the best educational institutions in North America under the guidance of Principal Charles Frederick Fraser. Fraser enacted a number of important educational innovations, including convincing the Nova Scotia Legislature to grant free education for the blind. As the only educational institute for the blind in the Maritimes, a major expansion took place in 1891 which added the new wing shown here on the right. Fraser remained principal until 1923 and was knighted for his tireless efforts in improving education for the blind.

Sacred Heart Convent c1915

Begun in 1851 as Halifax's first boarding school for girls, the Sacred Heart Convent was completed the next year. Initially the school was much smaller than what appears in this photograph. The convent's location at 5820 Spring Garden Road was still part of the undeveloped South Commons in 1850, yet the Sisters of the Sacred Heart were able to convince the authorities that their Brookside building (Lord Nelson Hotel site) was inadequate for a boarding school. Gradual expansion allowed the three-storey structure to accommodate a large number of girls. The Halifax Explosion destroyed the windows but left the wooden structure intact. The school is still in operation today.

Ladies College c1915

This institution of learning, affiliated with Dalhousie University, included an Art Studio as well as a Conservatory of Music and prepared students for university or a professional career in music. Located on Barrington Street at Harvey Street, the college had residential accommodations for about 100 students. Its total enrolment at the turn of the century under President Rev. Robert Laing was reported as 465 students.

Technical College c1912

The Technical College of Nova Scotia was built on the former site of the Militia Drill Shed at Spring Garden Road and Queen Street. In 1908 the Technical College was erected to serve as Nova Scotia's engineering school for research and degree programs. Six faculty taught the early engineering courses. In 1910, the first nine degrees were awarded. This structure is now occupied by the Faculty of Architecture.

Dalhousie College c1908

This red brick structure known as the Forrest Building was constructed in 1888 on the north east corner of Morris and Robie Streets, behind the old Exhibition Building. The first Dalhousie College opened on the Grand Parade, in 1820 with the assistance of the Earl of Dalhousie, but moved to this west end location, now called the Forrest Campus, when the City Fathers demanded the original site for a city hall. By the early 1900s, Dalhousie had become an important educational institution with almost four hundred students and thirty professors and lecturers.

• EDWARDIAN HALIFAX •

University of Kings College, Halifax, Nova Scotia, Canada. 21   A. R. Cogswell & Co. Photo

University of Kings College c1930

In 1929 the cornerstone of this Italian Renaissance structure was laid, and the following year King's College reopened on the Studley Campus in association with Dalhousie University. The original college, established at Windsor in 1789, was destroyed by fire and the college subsequently moved to temporary quarters in the Birchdale Hotel near the Northwest Arm. During the Second World War, King's became a naval officers' training facility, and the college relocated to Pine Hill.

• CHAPTER SIX •

Military Scenes

"Halifax sits on her hills by the sea
In the might of her pride,-
Invincible, terrible beautiful, she
With a sword at her side."

Pauline Johnson,
The Guard of the Eastern Gate

The Naval College c1912

When the Royal Navy quit Halifax in 1905, most of the buildings of the Royal Dockyard were closed, including the Naval Hospital that had been constructed in the North End behind Admiralty House in 1863. In 1911 this red sandstone building became the site of the Royal Naval College of Canada with a class of twenty-one cadets. Two years later, the first graduated naval officers were assigned to military duties. The Naval College was badly damaged during the Halifax Explosion, and the cadets were transferred to Kingston, Ontario. In 1918, the college was permanently moved to Esquimalt, British Columbia.

British Fleet in Halifax Harbour c1901

This picture was taken in October 1901 by the Notman Studio of Halifax. HMCS *Psyche* loads coal at Wharf 4 of the dockyard. Behind her, HMCS *Crescent* flies the Admiralty's flag. Coal was loaded on ships by hand in 1901, and the task was considered by naval crews to be one of the dirtiest and least desirable. Since Canada was still without its own navy, the British Fleet continued to patrol Canadian waters after Confederation and returned to Halifax each year. In 1910, the Naval Service of Canada came into existence and the following year, two ships were purchased creating Canada's Navy, one of which was the HMCS *Niobe*, visible here on the right, farthest out in the harbour.

The Armouries c1905

Recently declared a National Historic Site, the construction of the Armouries began in 1895 out of a block of slums and old shanties on North Park Street between Cunard Street and John's Lane. Stone from Pictou County and pressed brick from Elmsdale constituted the main building materials. The Armouries replaced a wooden drill shed that had been used for decades on Spring Garden Road near Queen Street.

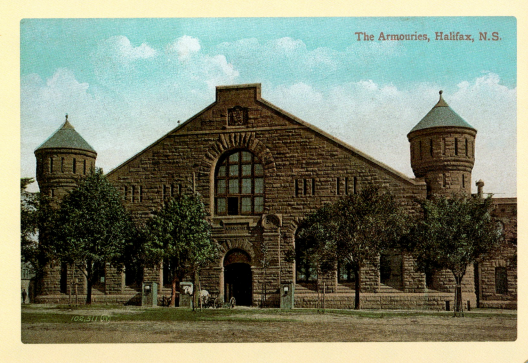

Church Parade at Garrison Chapel c1907

Located on the north-west corner of Brunswick and Cogswell Streets, Garrison Chapel was erected in 1844 and hosted the soldiers of the Wellington Barracks, Artillery Park, and the Citadel every Sunday morning until 1905. Outfitted in their scarlet uniforms, the soldiers would march accompanied by a military band and the colourful spectacle would end promptly at midday with the firing of the noon gun. The wooden structure was destroyed by fire in 1929.

Martello Tower c1910

The first Martello Tower to be constructed in the British Empire—the Prince of Wales Tower—was built by Prince Edward, Duke of Kent, to overlook the entrance to Halifax Harbour at Point Pleasant. This coastal defence tower was completed in 1799 on the highest point within Point Pleasant Park and was considered impregnable at the time. Many more similar towers were erected throughout the British Empire, including four more within the Halifax defence system.

Firing Salute on Citadel Hill c1907

Military regulations called for returning gun for gun all salutes from foreign warships in the harbour. Reverberations of the cannons echoed throughout the downtown when foreign ships visited Halifax since a twenty-one gun salute was standard naval procedure and, of course, a twenty-one return fire from the Citadel was mandatory. Agitation among the city's merchants often followed a grand firing since store windows often rumbled and sometimes shattered along Brunswick Street.

Entrance to Citadel c1910

Four soldiers stand guard at the Citadel. For those among the rank and file, life was an endurance test of boredom and bad food during peacetime and a survival test in wartime. Halifax and the Citadel flourished during war and declined during peace; however, a soldier's existence guarding the Citadel remained a constant diet of poor food, meagre pay, and monotonous routines often combined with ruthless discipline. Prisoners of war were held inside the Citadel, including one of Halifax's most famous visitors, Leon Trotsky, who was detained in March 1917.

Interior of Citadel c1905

A military exercise shows naval and army personnel accompanied by a garrison band. The picture faces east with the main entrance on the right and the signal masts flying on the south-east corner of the Citadel. As early as 1791 under the rule of Prince Edward, Duke of Kent, an impressive military telegraph system of flags, telescopes, and various signalling stations allowed messages to be received up to a distance of 17 mi. (27 km) and allowed the Prince to send communication from the Citadel as far as Annapolis Royal.

One O'clock Gun c1912

Regular firing from the Citadel's signal guns reminded citizens that Halifax was indeed a garrison town and they should regulate their watches. The discharge was a welcome sound for Haligonians, particularly on days that the Old Town Clock was not working. Each day a gun was fired at noon and nine-thirty at night. Special firings occurred often, including this one o'clock discharge on the Saluting Battery, facing the harbour outside the Citadel walls.

Melville Island at Night c1906

The 4-acre (1.6-ha) site in the Northwest Arm had a military prison, constructed in 1809 during the Napoleonic Wars, to house French prisoners. At the time, the island's isolation from downtown Halifax was considered ideal for a prison. A bridge on the south side connected the island to the mainland. In addition to the prison, a hospital and jailer's quarters, complete with lodging for an interpreter, were built on the island. Eventually Melville Prison became obsolete, and prisoners were transferred to Rockhead Prison in the North End. Today Melville Island is host to the Armdale Yacht Club.

Three War Monuments c1912

As the world drifted toward world war during the closing of the Edwardian age, people began to comprehend the consequences, horrors, and terrible suffering of modern warfare. This postcard shows the three sober monuments that recognize the most significant military operations involving the City of Halifax during the nineteenth century. The Martello Tower is a reminder of the War of 1812, the Sebastopol Monument of the Crimean War, and the South African Monument commemorates the Boer War.

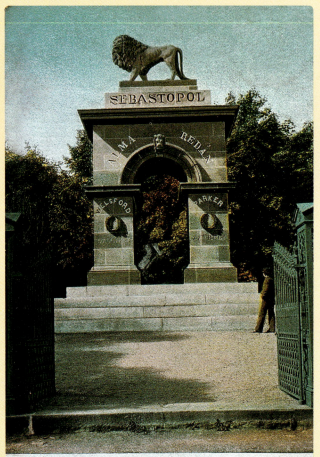

SEBASTOPOL MONUMENT OPPOSITE GOVERNEMENT HOUSE.
BARRINGTON ST.   HALIFAX, N.S.

Sebastopol Monument c1907

Erected in 1860 within the gates of St. Paul's Cemetery on Barrington Street, the Sebastopol Monument was constructed of red sandstone and lavishly restored in 1947. The arch with its massive lion was raised in memory of two Haligonians who died in the Crimean War: Captain William Parker and Major Augustus Welsford. Many of the first settlers as well as early soldiers and sailors were buried here, opposite Government House. For more than a century no new interments have been added to the historic cemetery.

• CHAPTER SEVEN •

Public Gardens and other Parks

"The inhabitants of Halifax took great pride in the charming expanse of trees and greenery of the Public Gardens which they considered the finest on the North American continent."

Phyllis R. Blakeley,
Glimpses of Halifax

The Lake, Public Gardens c1904

The "porthole and lantern" series of patriotic postcards were produced throughout the British Empire in the early 1900s with local scenes inserted into the porthole. This postcard concept proved popular in the Maritimes, and others were produced featuring nautical themes. This picture reveals a miniature sailboat afloat in Griffin's Pond. The pond was named for a young Irishman who was hanged nearby during the 1830s for murdering a man by a blow to the head with a lead pipe.

In the Gardens c1920

Victorian gardens are rare in Canada, and one of the most famous is Halifax's Public Gardens. Two young children approach one of the two bridges within the gardens that span Freshwater Brook on its path south-east to the harbour. The beautiful surrounding foliage includes more than eighty native and exotic kinds of trees and more than three hundred varieties of shrubs and flowers. The unique heritage gardens were recently declared a National Historic Site.

The Lake, Public Gardens c1908

This tiny lake called Griffin's Pond, with its man-made island for nesting wildfowl, was part of Freshwater Brook that began in a bog on Windsor Street near St. Mattias' Church. The brook ran across the North Commons and under Sackville Street into the miniature lake where it emptied out into a stream that flowed under Spring Garden Road west of the South Park Street intersection. Running along the eastern edge of Victoria Park, Freshwater Brook joined another stream from the upper end of South Street and the two streams flowed towards the harbour. Today the brook is visible only within the Public Gardens.

The Swans, Public Gardens c1926

The gardens' first swans, a white and black pair, were presented in 1877 by English benefactors. The two swans shown here were presented by King George V in 1926, and ever since swans have graced Griffin's Pond. Development of the Public Gardens began near Spring Garden Road, but the north side remained neglected until 1866 when the unsightly dumping grounds were gradually transformed into landscaped gardens. The pond was also transformed from an ugly square with walls into the charming circular lake seen here.

White Path, Public Gardens c1907

The Nova Scotia Horticultural Society first developed Halifax's Public Gardens on the South Commons along Spring Garden Road in 1836 as a 5-acre (2-ha) horticultural garden that promised to be "accessible to all classes." The Victorian era and its industrial revolution had produced considerable pollution and pandemonium. Consequently, urban gardens were laid out in the industrial British cities as rest areas for weary citizens. Halifax followed suit; the horticultural gardens were purchased by the city in 1874 and formally laid out as a Victorian botanical retreat by its first superintendent, Richard Power.

Public Gardens Seen Against Citadel Hill c1907

Looking north-east to Citadel Hill, one of Canada's first indoor skating rinks, which was constructed in 1863, stood at the site on the right near South Park Street. The rink was torn down in 1889, and indoor winter skating moved to the Exhibition Rink in the Exhibition Building on Tower Road. By the 1890s, costumed skating parties had become fashionable winter affairs. The Public Gardens became the location for other popular sports, including lawn tennis which was played on the public lawn area, the site of the earliest known court in Canada.

• Public Gardens and other Parks •

BAND STAND IN PUBLIC GARDENS.

Soldier's Fountain in Public Gardens, Halifax

Bandstand, Public Gardens
c1910

This ornate bandstand in the centre of the Public Gardens was erected in 1887 in honour of Queen Victoria's Golden Jubilee. Almost five thousand citizens flocked to the gardens to celebrate the famous Jubilee with a concert by various garrison bands as well as a display of fireworks. The bandstand became a popular site for outdoor musical events during the late 1800s and early 1900s.

Soldier's Fountain, Public Gardens
c1906

To commemorate Canada's role in the Boer War, this Soldier's Memorial Fountain was erected in 1903 with many interesting features at the fountain's base, including finely detailed water babies. The Boer War marked Canada's first major involvement in an overseas battle, and a number of Boer War monuments were erected throughout Halifax, including the South African Soldier's Monument on the grounds of Province House.

• EDWARDIAN HALIFAX •

Egg Pond, the Commons c1910

On the southern end of the North Commons between Bell Road and Cogswell Street, Egg Pond remained for many years a sizable natural lagoon of Freshwater Brook that had been landscaped and maintained as a duck pond and winter skating rink. The Halifax Commons had once been open fields from Cunard Street to South Street, but by 1900 much of the land south of Sackville Street had been developed. The North Commons, however, remained a playground for Haligonians throughout the twentieth century.

Prince's Lodge c1907

A view of the lodge from Bedford Basin shows the music rotunda, the only remaining structure of a grand lodge built by Prince Edward during his residence at Halifax between 1794 and 1800. The Georgian rotunda was used by Edward and his mistress Julie Saint Laurent to host musical concerts with performances by the Prince's Regimental Band. Nearby at Hemlock Ravine Park is a remodelled heart-shaped pond named for Julie that evokes the historical romance.

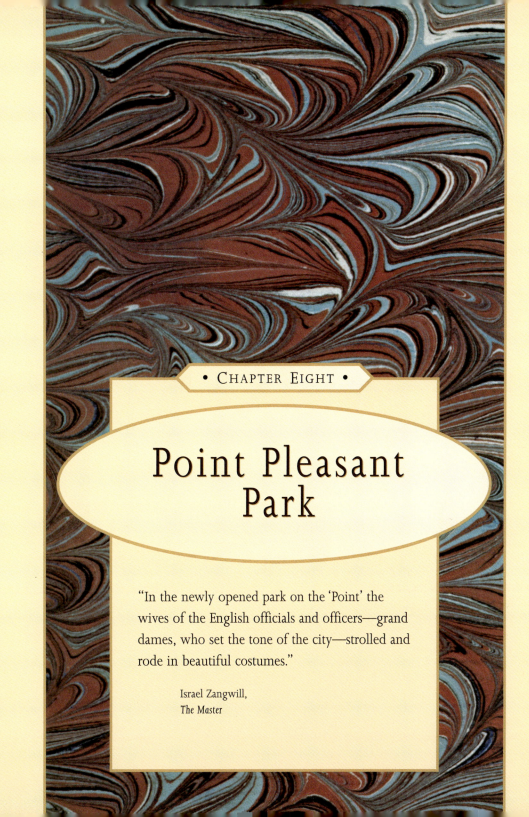

• CHAPTER EIGHT •

Point Pleasant Park

"In the newly opened park on the 'Point' the wives of the English officials and officers—grand dames, who set the tone of the city—strolled and rode in beautiful costumes."

Israel Zangwill,
The Master

Pleasant Street from Greenbank c1909

Pleasant Street led from the downtown across the "Kissing Bridge" at the bottom of Inglis Street where Freshwater Brook ran into the harbour. Eventually industries on Pleasant Street included a lime kiln, a brewery, Baker's Lobster Factory, a lumberyard, and the Chebucto Foundry. Shown here is the harbour road to Point Pleasant Park, with the Royal Nova Scotia Yacht Squadron on the right.

The Greenbank Entrance to Point Pleasant Park c1907

The shore road entrance to Point Pleasant Park from Pleasant Street was near present-day Black Rock Beach. On the left is Steele's Pond, a popular winter skating site where sixteen-year-old Amy Boutillier and her friend drowned one January when their horse and sleigh went through the ice. This tranquil view has been infilled and now comprises the southern section of the Ocean Terminals complex.

Greenbank c1910

A popular day-long outing for Haligonians in the early 1900s, before the motor era, was a round trip along the South End peninsula, either walking or by carriage, through Greenbank, Point Pleasant, along the Northwest Arm, and back to the city. Favourite rest spots had benches installed, such as this comfortable site at Greenbank just north of Point Pleasant Park. By 1900, the prosperous seaport had its open spaces and playgrounds dressed up to create beautiful cultivated areas for the citizens.

Greenbank, Another View c1910

The same site as in the previous scene offers a view south into Point Pleasant Park. At the time, few homes had been constructed this far south but between World Wars I and II, homes were built nearby to house dock workers. Many of these homes were later expropriated to make way for the Ocean Terminals development.

• Edwardian Halifax •

Entrance to Park c1906

This photograph shows the Young Avenue entrance with its antique Golden Gates heading southwest, into Point Pleasant Park along the same pathway that exists today. These beautiful gates were constructed in Dartmouth by the Starr Manufacturing Company, which was famous for developing the world's first steel skate. In the early 1900s, Point Pleasant Drive did not run along the edge of the Park perpendicular to Young Avenue, nor did the beautiful fountain found today exist yet at this site.

Exit from Park along Young Avenue c1906

This scene shows the old park gates that exited from Point Pleasant along Young Avenue towards the city. Although the north end of Young Avenue and South Park Street contained some of the city's finest homes and most splendidly designed grounds by the early 1900s, this southernmost end of Young Avenue remained undeveloped.

Inside the Gates at Park Keeper's House c1908

Constructed in 1896, the park keeper's house on the right is located near the Young Avenue entrance, visible in the background. Further up and to the right is Quarry Pond. June foliage embellishes the surrounding hardwoods. Away from the downtown smoke and soot, the people of Edwardian Halifax were fortunate to have a wilderness park so close.

Quarry Pond, Point Pleasant Park c1908

Quarry Pond is located just above the Golden Gates entrance at Young Avenue. It supplied building stones to construction sites in pioneer Halifax town. Quarry Pond was one of many popular outdoor natural skating rinks that graced Halifax one hundred years ago. Today Quarry Pond is the sole outdoor winter skating spot in peninsular Halifax.

Scenic Road along the Point c1906

The southern tip of the peninsula of Halifax was known as Tower Woods after the military completed Martello Tower in 1798. In 1866 the Imperial authorities offered 186 acres (75 ha) of forest to the city for an annual fee of one shilling per year. In the 1870s, Tower Woods became Point Pleasant Park as the military gradually cut splendid roads and scenic paths throughout the seaside sanctuary.

Point Pleasant with Halifax in Background c1906

About 1762, Point Pleasant became a fortified deforested area studded with forts and sea batteries that provided a coastal defence system against incoming enemy vessels. After its military installations became obsolete by the mid-1800s, forests were no longer cut back and this tranquil nature retreat with the panoramic view became a favourite escape for residents of Victorian Halifax. This picture was taken near Black Rock Beach on the harbour side of the park. North in the distance lies Halifax.

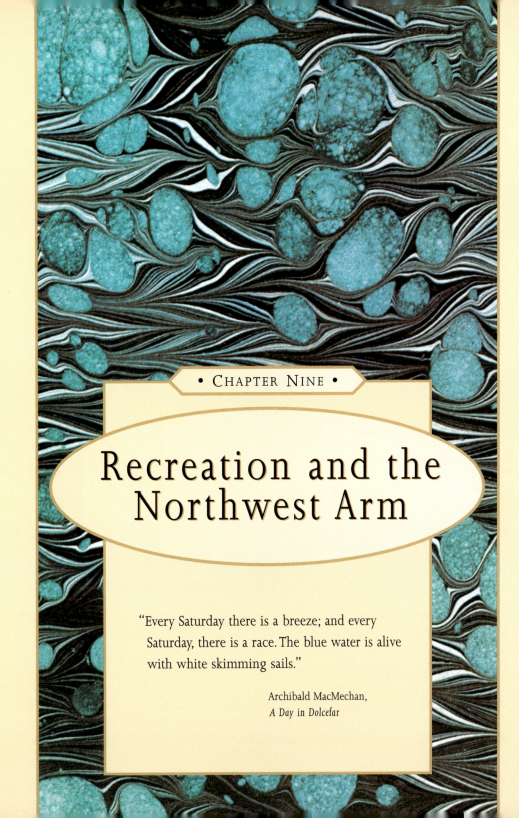

• CHAPTER NINE •

Recreation and the Northwest Arm

"Every Saturday there is a breeze; and every Saturday, there is a race. The blue water is alive with white skimming sails."

Archibald MacMechan,
A Day in Dolcefar

Royal Nova Scotia Yacht Squadron, Halifax, Nova Scotia. 9

Royal Nova Scotia Yacht Squadron (RNSYS) c1940

This picture was taken from the harbour showing the RNSYS's clubhouse and boathouse near Black Rock Beach. Point Pleasant Park is in the background. The oldest yacht club in North America traces its roots to the Royal Halifax Yacht Club in Halifax's North End. In 1890 the RNSYS established a clubhouse in the South End, which was demolished during World War I to make way for the Ocean Terminals. The clubhouse pictured here was opened in 1922 and abandoned in 1971 for a new site on the Northwest Arm.

Pilot Boats at Anchor, Purcell's Cove, Halifax, N.S.

Pilot Boats at Anchor, Purcell's Cove c1910

A picturesque scene on the Arm bears the following enigmatic but romantic inscription:
"Remember the present-
Remember the past-
Remember the boy-
that kissed you last....
A Friend"

Purcell's Cove c1910

This view overlooks Spectacle Island and the Northwest Arm. Purcells Cove and the Cox Quarry (sometimes called Queen's Quarry) at Bluestone, near the entrance to the Northwest Arm, was an important source for Halifax's early building stones. For years a ferry at Point Pleasant Park allowed residents of the cove and the western side of the Arm to cross to Halifax.

Scene on Northwest Arm c1906

A typical fall day on the Northwest Arm at the turn of the century is tranquil after summer activities die down. Boating and regattas, bathing and picnics became favourite pastimes for Haligonians at the Arm before motorcars in the 1920s would carry them away from the crowds to the more secluded South Shore.

A Scene on the Beautiful Northwest Arm c1912

Across the Arm from the mainland, the Northwest Arm Rowing Clubhouse is visible. Once Halifax entered the automobile age in the 1920s, the popularity of the Arm faded. As Thomas Raddall remarked in Halifax, *The Warden of the North*, "The old aquatic spectacles of the nineties and the Edwardian years, the smart military bands playing at the Waegwoltic, and the whole Arm covered with energetic young men in flannels and girls with parasols— these were a thing of the past."

The Memorial Tower c1930

Fleming Park and the Memorial Tower can be seen from the Northwest Arm. The great railway builder Sir Sandford Fleming donated 100 acres (40 ha) for a natural park in 1908. Four years later, with assistance from Halifax's Canadian Club, the Memorial Tower was erected to commemorate the 150th anniversary of the birth of Representative Government in the British Empire.

Regatta, Northwest Arm c1910

This view looking south-east shows one of the many boating regattas held at the Northwest Arm Rowing Club from 1899. During the first decade of the twentieth century, the Northwest Arm Rowing Clubhouse was considered the largest and most extensively equipped boathouse in Canada. Both rowing and sailing events were held during the regattas. Clubs from Halifax Harbour and Dartmouth lakes as well as other Arm clubs, such as the St. Mary's A. A. and Aquatic Club, often contested the meets.

Regatta, North-West Arm, Halifax, N.S.

The Waegwoltic Club c1932

"Waegwoltic" is the name given to the Northwest Arm by the Mi'kmaq. In 1908 the Waegwoltic Club opened its doors as a combined boating and country club for families. Located on the eastern shore of the Arm at the bottom of Coburg Road, Waegwoltic was acquired from the A. G. Jones estate that once belonged to Richard Uniacke. Ideally situated on the most beautiful section of the Arm and open year-round, Waegwoltic quickly became Halifax's most fashionable resort. Its first President was John W. Regan who, in 1908, wrote the definitive history of the waterway: *Sketches and Traditions of the Northwest Arm*.

THE WAEGWOLTIC, NORTH WEST ARM, HALIFAX, N. S.

• EDWARDIAN HALIFAX •

Swimming at Boat Club c1909

Public bathing establishments opened in 1898 along the harbour at Greenbank and in the North End below the Wellington Barracks. It was years later before the Public Baths at Armview opened along the Northwest Arm. This scene appears to have been taken at the Northwest Arm Rowing Club where a lone swimmer takes to the water, encouraged by onlookers from the club's balcony.

Northwest Arm Rowing Club c1908

Located at Cunard's Wharf near the foot of South Street, the Northwest Arm Rowing Club was the pioneer boat club on the Arm. Organized in 1899, the club offered almost two hundred berths in its boathouse, membership at the club was well subscribed. The club experienced instant financial success so the boathouse was enlarged and remained the largest on the Arm. Robinson's Ferry was always nearby to transport people across the Arm. Canoes for day-tripping became extremely fashionable in the late 1800s. Canoe races and regattas involving other small pleasure craft often added to the gaiety.

Boat Club, Northwest Arm c1910

This card bears a short note to Miss W. Edwards 135 Victor Ave, Toronto, Ont: "This is where we have our Regattas. I suppose you heard about our beautiful Northwest Arm. Arthur."

The Head of Northwest Arm c1920

Eventually a bridge was constructed for travellers heading up the St. Margarets Bay Road or down the west side of the Arm. According to tradition, a beaver dam once existed here and there was great trout fishing, which may account for the belief that a significant Mi'kmaq camp was nearby.

THE RUN, HEAD OF NORTH WEST ARM — HALIFAX, N.S.

Published for C. H. Smith, Halifax, N.S. 1431

• EDWARDIAN HALIFAX •

North West Arm from the Memorial Tower, Halifax, Nova Scotia.—82.

Northwest Arm from the Memorial Tower c1940

The Northwest Arm is a lovely inlet that winds upland, creating the Halifax peninsula. Once a mecca for the Mi'kmaq to camp, hunt, and fish, the charm and quiet beauty of the Arm attracted the early Halifax gentry who established cottages and country estates in the area. The Edwardian era brought numerous boat clubs and bathhouses and thousands of people flocked here most weekends.

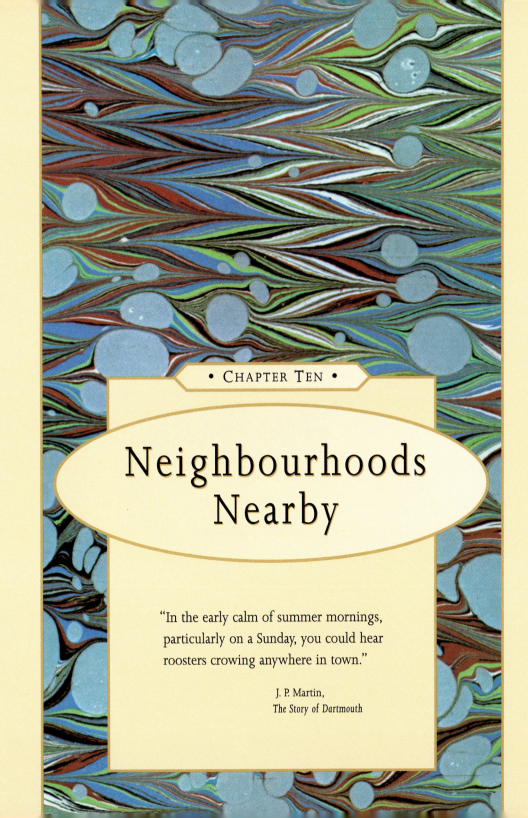

• CHAPTER TEN •

Neighbourhoods Nearby

"In the early calm of summer mornings, particularly on a Sunday, you could hear roosters crowing anywhere in town."

J. P. Martin,
The Story of Dartmouth

*A Picturesque Corner, Herring Cove
c1905*

Settled as early as 1752, Herring Cove's location at the entrance to Halifax Harbour made the small cove an important part of the Halifax coastal defence system. Nearby York Redoubt and later the naval radio station at Camperdown were vital links to Halifax's military establishment. Besides fishing, residents of Herring Cove made their living supplying the military fortifications. The small Herring Cove Anglican Church was used as the village classroom until 1878, when the community built its first school.

Dartmouth, Looking to the Entrance of Halifax Harbour c1906

This view is from "The Brae," an elaborate estate on Cleveland Crescent. The postcard was published about 1906 by Canadian Souvenir Cards, but the picture may have been photographed several years earlier. The large wooden building near the outflow from Sullivan's Pond is the Starr Manufacturing plant. The large structure to the right is Octagon House. Located at Dahlia and Oak Streets, the residence was known locally as the "ink bottle house." It was constructed in 1871 for Gavin Holiday of the Starr Manufacturing Company. This unique building had three stories with a crowning cupola and remained a landmark in downtown Dartmouth until 1969, when it was removed for the construction of a high-rise.

Bird's-Eye View of Dartmouth c1912

This picture of downtown Dartmouth was taken near the entrance to Alderney Drive at Geary Street. A large schooner and Dartmouth Cove are in the background. Near this scene Dartmouth's first industry, a sawmill operation, was established in 1749. Three years later a ferry service came into operation, and for the next two hundred years, Dartmouth remained a small close-knit community supplying raw materials and manufactured goods to Halifax and other parts of Nova Scotia.

Dartmouth, View from the Park c1910

The town of Dartmouth had grown steadily during the late 1800s and was incorporated in 1873. This view is from the Dartmouth Commons towards Fairy Hill, where the small pavilion known as the Summer-House was constructed in 1890. Behind the hill at Edward and Park Streets, iron ore was mined by John Cleverdon in the 1840s. The ferry approaching the Dartmouth terminal is probably the Scottish built *Chebucto*, but two other ferries also worked the harbour during this period—the *Dartmouth* and the *Halifax*. In May 1909 the first commutation for autos was set at twenty-five cents per one-way fare.

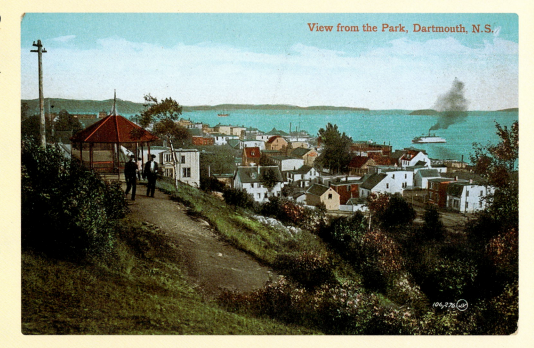

Halifax from Dartmouth Park c1910

This picture was taken from the Dartmouth Commons. Symonds' Foundry is on the right at the harbour. Established by James Greig, the foundry produced stoves, furnaces, water pipes, propellers, and ship machinery. Adjoining the foundry on the left is the fashionable residence of W. S. Symonds, Dartmouth's first mayor. The original meeting of the town's first council was held here in 1873. Opposite Symonds' house heading east is the boat shop of noted boat builder E. F. Williams.

The Ferry Landing, Dartmouth c1912

The Dartmouth Ferry Waiting Room was built in 1906 to replace the old one. The new terminal remained a fixture on the Dartmouth side until the 1980s. The ferry shown here is probably the *Dartmouth*. Built in Yarmouth in 1888 and nicknamed the *Old Veteran*, it remained in service for almost fifty years, until it was sold for scrap in 1935. The picture shows a new walkway that had just been completed. The last wagon on the left would be delivering milk to Halifax.

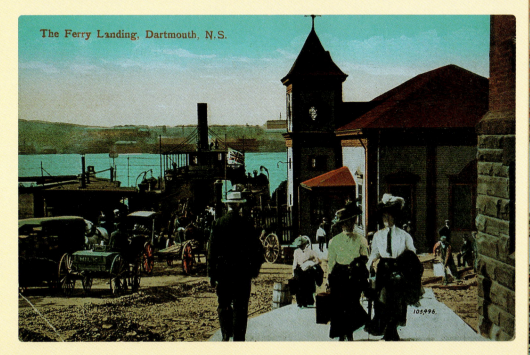

• EDWARDIAN HALIFAX •

Banook Canoe Club, Dartmouth. N.S.

Banook Canoe Club c1912

Nova Scotia's first canoe club was established in 1902 and incorporated the following year with a boathouse and canoe shed. The main clubhouse shown here was erected in 1904 and still stands today. The club assumed responsibility for the annual Natal Regatta and became an important source for the development of Canadian competitive canoeing. Except for the war years, races were held annually throughout the summer months. A new development occurred in 1920 when large war canoes with twelve paddlers proved popular with spectators as well as the media and aided the development of paddling on the Dartmouth lakes.

A Glimpse of the Lakes, Dartmouth, N.S.

A Glimpse of the Lakes, Dartmouth c1910

This picture was taken along Waverly Road, near today's Micmac Parclo, looking towards one of the islands on Lake Micmac. Even today, this scene is familiar since Lake Micmac's western shore is still pristine. The lake was part of the Shubenacadie Canal system as well as an important source for Dartmouth's ice business, which was exported to New York and New England before artificial ice became commercially feasible.

Bedford at Lister's Bridge c1909

A scene from the Fort Sackville grounds spans south along the Shore Road. Lister's Bridge, in the foreground, was the site of a controversial toll gate that was attacked and destroyed by mounted gunmen in 1782. The toll gate and its keeper were continually assaulted and reprimanded by travellers until tolls were removed. The small building on the road to the right is the Ennis cottage.

Bedford at Night c1911

This night scene offers the same view as the previous postcard. On the far right is the embankment of the overhead railroad line. Situated at the head of the Bedford Basin and the mouth of the Sackville River, Bedford was a crossroads for the Mi'kmaq and early French explorers. The English, led by Captain Gorham, established Fort Sackville in 1749 to secure the entire harbour and basin of Chebucto for settlement. Gradually, roads and bridges were constructed between Halifax, Windsor, and Truro that maintained Bedford's role as the crossroads for Nova Scotians travelling inland.

• Edwardian Halifax •

Bedford Railway Bridge c1910

A scene from the Bedford Highway across the Sackville River to the Railway Bridge and the Shore Road shows Lister's Bridge and the head of Bedford Basin. In 1857 the railroad from Richmond Station in north end Halifax to this point at Bedford was completed. The following year, it was extended to Windsor and Truro. Behind the left embankment where the railway bridge touches land is the approximate site of Scott Manor House.

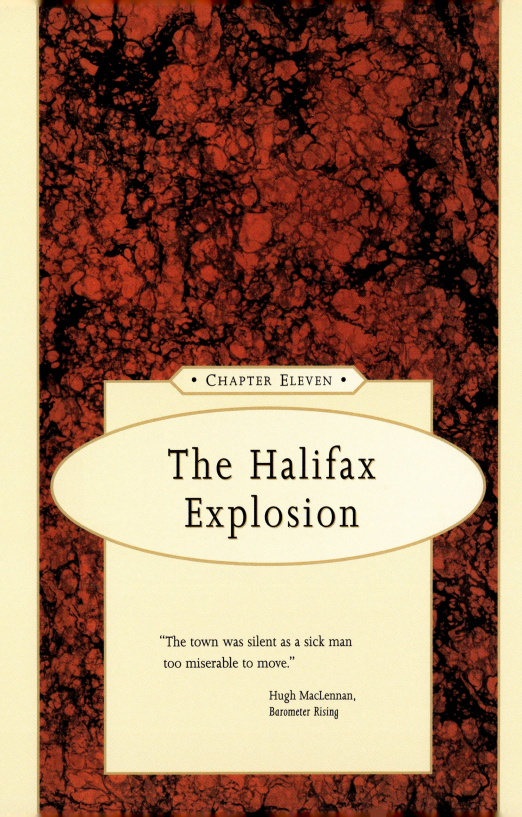

• CHAPTER ELEVEN •

The Halifax Explosion

"The town was silent as a sick man too miserable to move."

Hugh MacLennan,
Barometer Rising

Collision of this Vessel the "S.S. Imo" with "Mont Blanc" Caused Great Halifax Disaster
—Copyright Underwood & Underwood, N.Y.

Collision of the Imo with Mont Blanc c1917

Postcards of the Halifax Explosion were photographed on the spot and issued instantly in black and white. Here is one of the best-known pictures that shows the Belgian relief steamer *Imo* lying on the Dartmouth shore—the vessel was in mid-harbour when the *Mont Blanc* exploded. Armed guards were placed nearby to stand watch against looters. Four months later, the 5,043-ton vessel was refloated and taken to New York for repairs. It eventually returned to sea for a short time as a whale oil tanker.

Actual View of Section of Halifax Harbor where Explosion Occurred, and "S.S. Imo" in Background
—Copyright Underwood & Underwood, N.Y.

Halifax Harbour where Explosion Occurred c1917

A scene from the dockyard above the harbour between Richmond and North Street shows the *Imo* lying stranded on its side at Dartmouth's Black Rock Point. The *Mont Blanc* was blown to bits; the *Imo* took the blast head-on, killing the captain and a number of the vessel's crew. Massive devastation occurred on both sides of the harbour.

Halifax Railroad Station c1917

Captured in this picture is the city's only railroad station at the foot of North Street after it was destroyed by the full impact of the blast. The glass and iron roof collapsed into the platforms and tracks, killing sixty people throughout the terminus. The railroad yard surrounding the station was also destroyed; shattered railway cars and tracks littered the North End. (A photograph in chapter three shows this railroad station prior to the explosion.) Halifax's railroad terminus was moved to the South End near the Ocean Terminals.

Halifax Railroad Station, in which 60 Persons were killed by falling roof.
—Copyright Underwood & Underwood, N.Y.

Oland Breweries, Dartmouth c1917

Shown here near Tufts Cove in north end Dartmouth are the remains of the sprawling Oland Breweries. Seven employees were killed, including the manager and Conrad Oland. This structure, erected in 1896 to replace an older building had its own rail spur and private wharf. The breweries never re-opened here. North of the breweries, a Mi'kmaq settlement was flattened by the explosion, and the few surviving members of the Turtle Grove band permanently fled the harbour site.

Terrible Halifax Disaster. Olands' Breweries Completely Destroyed.

View of Wreckage from Halifax Disaster—Copyright Underwood & Underwood, N.Y.

View of Wreckage c1917

This view shows soldiers searching among the ruins of the Hillis & Sons Foundry near Pier eight at Richmond. Of the forty-three employees who reported to work on December 6, 1917, only two survived, including fifteen-year-old Frank Burford whose father perished inside the foundry. Besides the foundry, Richmond's other major industries—the Acadia Sugar Refinery and the Richmond Printing Company—were also destroyed in the explosion. In fact, all buildings in Richmond were destroyed by the blast.

Snow-covered Devastated Residential Section of Halifax, after Terrible Explosion —Copyright Underwood & Underwood, N.Y.

Devastated Residential Section c1917

The day after the terrible explosion, an equally dreadful snowstorm covered the ruins. The Halifax Explosion was the largest man-made explosion before Hiroshima and its death toll made it one of the greatest disasters in Canadian history. More than sixteen hundred people, including five hundred children, lost their lives. The impact of the blast was felt a 100 mi. (161 km) in every direction and was even felt in Cape Breton, more than 200 mi. (322 km) away. The north ends of Halifax and Dartmouth were wiped out, and few windows throughout Halifax were left intact.

Winter Scene in Halifax c1917

"Barbara could see the heavy snowfall from the hospital window." Survivor Barbara Orr was fourteen at the time of the Halifax Explosion. She recalled the day after in the book Survivors: Children of the Halifax Explosion.

Conclusion: Halifax 1920

Though optimism, progress, and faith in technology characterized the onset of the Edwardian age in 1901, it ended in hardship and feelings of despair nearly twenty years later. Halifax, in particular, had experienced a number of painful events in the period that made life in the port city the toughest in memory.

In 1906 the last of the Imperial troops left Halifax, which proved a terrible loss to the city both emotionally and economically since British forces had founded the city and purchased most of their supplies from Halifax merchants. Six years later the city witnessed the aftermath of the *Titanic* tragedy and buried many of the victims in its cemeteries. The apparent failure of what was considered the most advanced technology of the day shocked the world. The death toll during the First World War dampened any local enthusiasm for the prosperity that had resulted from the war in Halifax.

The appalling death and destruction of the Halifax Explosion in 1917—partly a result of careless storage of wartime munitions—inflicted tremendous suffering upon the port city. Further wartime misery resulted in 1918 when a servicemen's riot severely damaged the downtown.

Finally, as the troops and convoys abandoned Halifax to return to their hometowns across Canada, a post-war depression set in during 1920 that threatened to turn the Warden of the North into a ghost town. The exodus of people and businesses from Halifax and the rest of the Maritime Provinces happened well before the rest of North America noticed the negative effects of post-war inflation. For the first time in its history and despite normal birth rates, the population of Halifax stood still during the 1920s.

In effect, 1920 marked the end of the series of disasters that shook Halifax throughout the previous decade, yet economic calamities continued through the 1920s and well into the 1930s. The confidence and enthusiasm that had characterized the opening decade of the twentieth century had long vanished. During peacetime Halifax had always experienced economic adversity but nothing as severe as the poverty and unrest of the 1920s.

However, all was not lost. The trials of the fortress by the sea would eventually turn around via development as a national port with capacity for ocean liners and warships. Strategically located Halifax would once again flourish as a port during the next, even more ghastly, world war— a double-edged kind of prosperity that Haligonians knew well.

- CHAPTER TWELVE -

Edwardian Greeting Postcards

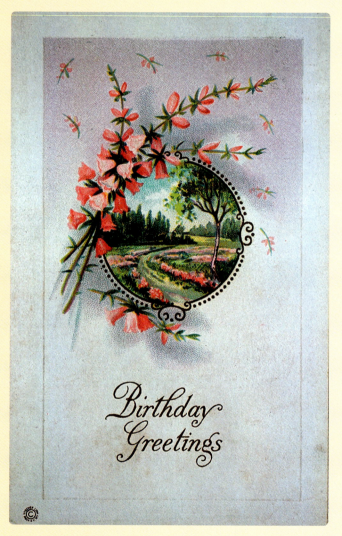

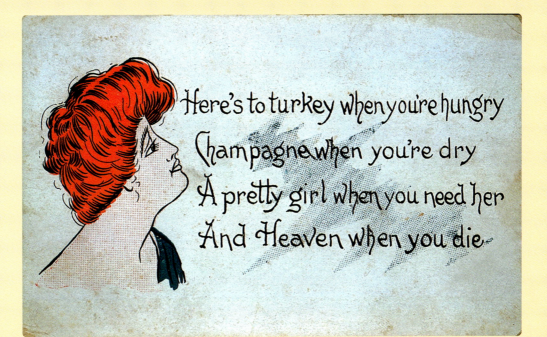

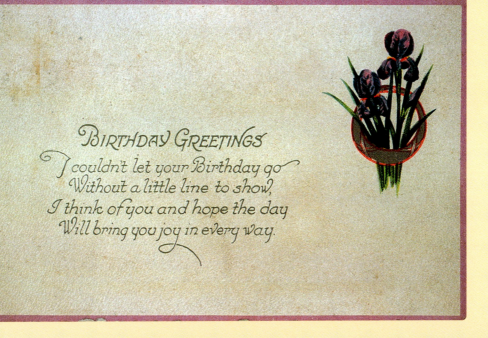

• Edwardian Halifax •